Ready, Steady, Practise!

Spelling
Pupil Book Year 3

Jon Goulding

Features of this book

- Clear explanations and worked examples for each spelling topic from the KS2 National Curriculum.

- Questions split into three sections that become progressively more challenging:

  Warm up

  Test yourself

  Challenge yourself

- 'How did you do?' checks at the end of each topic for self-evaluation.

- Regular progress tests to assess pupils' understanding and recap on their learning.

- Answers to every question in a pull-out section at the centre of the book.

Contents

Regular and irregular words	4
Long and short vowel sounds	6
Syllables	8
Making words plural	10
Suffixes 1: adding –er, –ed and –ing	12
Prefixes 1: un–, dis– and mis–	14
Progress tests 1 and 2	**16–17**
Plural endings	18
The suffix –ly	20
Words with ge and dge	22
–gue and –que from French	24
Words with ei, eigh and ey	26
Different spelling, same sound	28
Progress tests 3 and 4	**30–31**
Prefixes 2: A variety of meanings	32
ch from different languages	34
Using y to spell the short *i* sound	36
When ou spells the *u* sound	38
Homophones	40
Progress tests 5 and 6	**42–43**
Answers (centre pull-out)	**1–4**

Regular and irregular words

Many words are phonically **regular**. You can 'sound out' each phoneme in phonically regular words.

Lots of words are phonically **irregular** – the whole word cannot be sounded out using the individual letter sound.

Regular

bread

b-r-ea-d

The five letters give four sounds (phonemes).

Irregular

people

sounds a bit like

p-ee-p-ul

table

sounds a bit like

t-ay-bul

Warm up

1) The words below have been misspelt. Copy the lists of words, then match them to the correct spelling and practise writing the correct word.
An example has been done for you.

a) sed   people

b) beecuz   would

c) peepul   said

d) wud   mother

e) muther   because

f) litul   sandwich

g) sanwij   little

Test yourself

2 Look at the picture and write out each complete word with the correct phoneme.

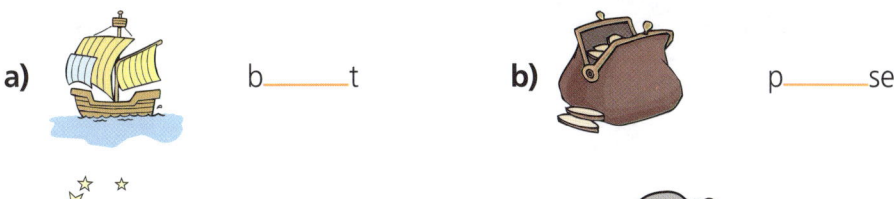

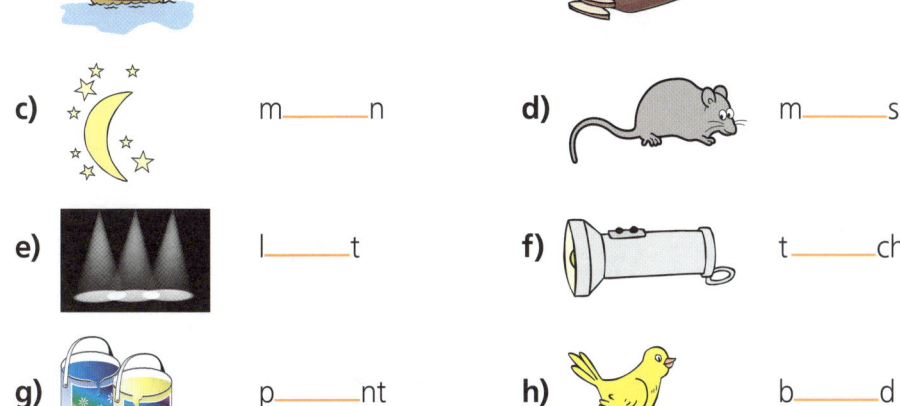

a) b_____t

b) p_____se

c) m_____n

d) m_____se

e) l_____t

f) t_____ch

g) p_____nt

h) b_____d

Challenge yourself

3 Choose the correct phonically irregular word from the list to complete each sentence.

| floor | shoes | pretty | climb |
| kind | laugh | hour | |

a) I have got new _____.

b) We tried to _____ the mountain.

c) The bride wore a very _____ wedding dress.

d) He was _____ to share.

e) The train arrives in one _____.

f) The plate smashed as it hit the _____.

g) The joke made us all _____.

How did you do?

Long and short vowel sounds

The phonemes in some words are spelt the same, but have different sounds.

Examples:

She is r**ea**ding a book.
This **ea** has a **long** vowel sound.

He bumped his h**ea**d.
This **ea** has a **short** vowel sound.

Sometimes a long vowel sound is split. The two vowels making the sound are separated by a consonant. The final vowel is an **e**.
Adding an **e** to the word **mad** creates a split long vowel sound made by the **a** and the **e** – **made** (a_e makes the *ay* or *ai* sound).

Warm up

1. Make some **ea** words with a **long** vowel sound. An example has been done for you.

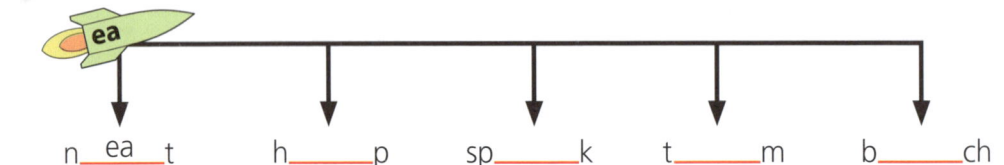

   n__ea__t   h____p   sp____k   t____m   b____ch

2. Write some **ea** words with a **short** vowel sound. An example has been done for you.

   thr__ea__d   d____f   sw____t   w____ther   m____dow

3. Make some **oo** words with a **long** vowel sound. An example has been done for you.

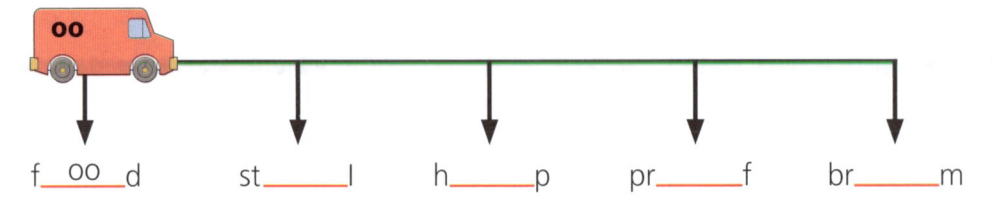

   f__oo__d   st____l   h____p   pr____f   br____m

4. Write some **oo** words with a **short** vowel sound. An example has been done for you.

   g__oo__d   b____k   f____t   st____d   sh____k

Test yourself

5 Copy each sentence and insert the missing letters to give the words a long vowel sound. An example has been done for you.

a) Dice are usually a c<u>ube</u> shape.

b) He r__d__ the horse along the lane.

c) The fruit was all r__p__.

d) The spy cracked the secret c__d__.

e) Water leaked from the p__p__.

f) Most of my class h__t__ cabbage.

g) The weather was f__n__.

h) The glass was polished to a brilliant sh__n__.

Challenge yourself

6 Find the vowel sounds for the words in bold.

Decide if each vowel sound is long, 'L' or short, 'S'.

> **Example**
>
>   L   L L
> The **team** scored a **late goal**.

a) It was a **hot day**.

b) **They made** a **den** in the garden.

c) **Rain** was **soaking** everyone.

d) The superhero **had** a **long flowing cape**.

e) She **went** for a **run** in the **park**.

How did you do?

Syllables

When you say a word **slowly**, you can hear how many **syllables** (or beats) it has. You can tap out the syllables of a word, as you say it, to help you. Breaking a word into its syllables can help you to spell it.

Example:

car

This has **one** syllable.

car - pet

This has **two** syllables.

car - pen - ter

This has **three** syllables.

Warm up

1. Say each word slowly. Copy each one and write the number of syllables.

modern	invade
cabin	king
determine	sport
together	introduce
industry	seat
expensive	September
travel	habit
method	direct
farm	bird

Test yourself

2 How many syllables are there in each word below?

century	decade
millennium	year
fortnight	eternity
forever	lifetime

Challenge yourself

3 Write the days of the week that contain:

a) two syllables

b) three syllables

4 Write the months of the year that contain:

a) only one syllable

b) two syllables

c) three syllables

d) four syllables

5 Write some words of your own with the correct number of syllables.

a) two syllables

b) three syllables

c) four syllables

d) five syllables

How did you do?

Making words plural

Singular means there is just **one** thing.
Plural means there is **more than one**.
Most nouns have a singular and a plural form.

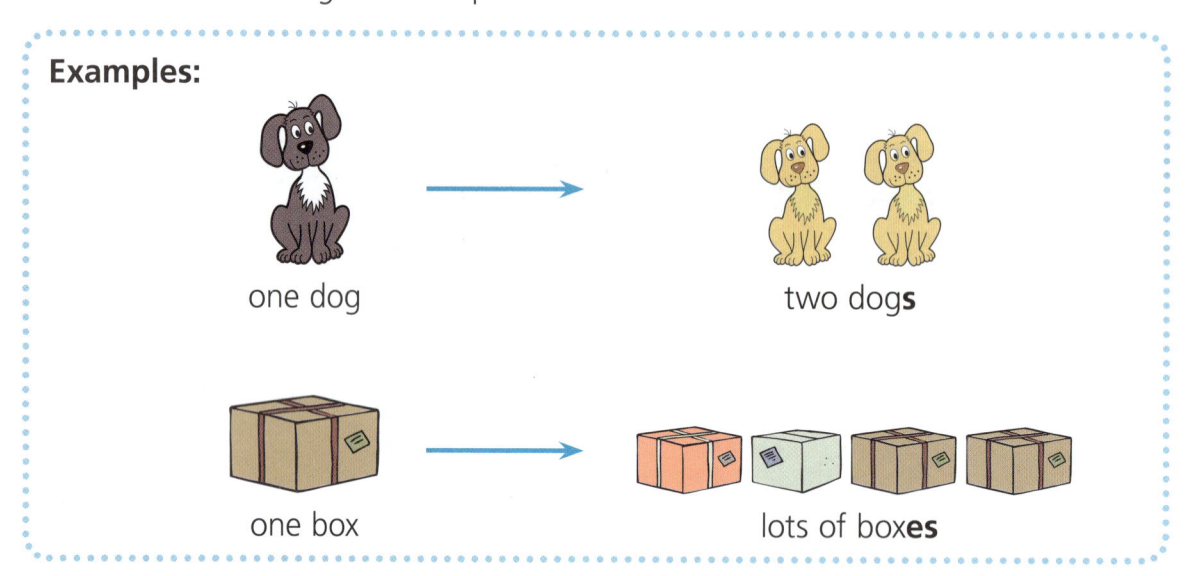

Examples:

one dog → two dog**s**

one box → lots of box**es**

You add **s** to most nouns to make them plural.
However, you add **es** to most nouns ending in **ch**, **sh**, **x** or **s**.

Warm up

1 Copy these tables and write the plural form of each noun.

An example has been done for you.

singular	plural
dish	dishes
kiss	
cat	
coach	
fox	
song	

singular	plural
boss	
tree	
six	
catch	
bus	
miss	

Test yourself

2 Copy and complete these phrases with the correct singular or plural form of the noun.

a) one dress, three _____

b) one bush, two _____

c) one _____, seven horses

d) one bench, two _____

e) one _____, three carpets

f) one window, five _____

g) one _____, three buses

h) one _____, four pizzas

Challenge yourself

3 Copy and complete each sentence below with a suitable word from the list. Remember to make the word plural before adding it.

splash   glass   sheep   moon   coach   potato   house   six

a) The children got _____ of paint on their clothes.

b) I saw many _____ at the farm.

c) Jupiter is a planet with many _____.

d) _____ are used for making crisps and chips.

e) Care is needed when washing _____.

f) We needed three _____ to take us on our school trip.

g) She was great at batting in cricket, and hit lots of _____.

h) Lots of new _____ were being built near to the school.

How did you do?

Suffixes 1: adding –er, –ed and –ing

A **suffix** is a group of letters that can be added to the end of some words to change their meanings. When a word has more than one syllable and ends in a consonant, you **sometimes** need to double the consonant before adding the suffix.

> **Examples:**
>
> begin – begi**nn**er   visit – visi**t**ing
>
> occur – occu**rr**ed   limit – limi**t**ed
>
> Here, the **last** syllable in the root word is stressed – a greater emphasis is placed on the **last** syllable when saying the word:
>
> begIN   ocCUR
>
> So, the consonant is **doubled**.
>
> Here, the **first** syllable in the root word is stressed – a greater emphasis is placed on the **first** syllable when saying the word:
>
> VISit   LIMit
>
> So, the consonant is **not doubled**.

If a word ends in **w**, **x** or **y** the consonant is not doubled, e.g. rela**x** – rela**x**ed, rela**x**ing.

Warm up

1 Write the words that **–er**, **–ed** and **–ing** can be added to.

Say the words to check that they make sense.

jump	cat	garden
call	camp	stairs

2 Write these words in the past tense by adding **–ed**. Decide whether you need to double the consonant.

prefer	visit
exclaim	hover
occur	beg

Test yourself

3) Correct the sentence by changing the underlined word to its correct form.

Look out for exceptions and words which require changing in a different way.

a) When I was in Year 1, I always <u>prefer</u> to have a hot school dinner.

b) Two years ago, the same argument always <u>occur</u> at the bus stop.

c) The children <u>beg</u> for every penny they raised.

d) There is a <u>limit</u> range of goods for sale.

e) The teenagers had trouble <u>admit</u> they were wrong.

f) Sunbathing is <u>relax</u>, but not if it is too hot.

Challenge yourself

4) Each of these words can have at least two of **–er**, **–ed** or **–ing** added.

Write two sentences for each root word. Each sentence must include the root word with a different ending.

a) relax

b) garden

c) begin

d) play

How did you do?

Prefixes 1: un-, dis- and mis-

A **prefix** is a group of letters that may be added to the beginning of a word. When you add a prefix it does not change the spelling of the root word, but it does change its meaning.

Examples:

well   **un**well   agree   **dis**agree   behave   **mis**behave

When you add the prefixes **un–** and **dis–**, they make the word mean the opposite. The prefix **mis–** often means wrong or something done badly.

Warm up

1 Copy the words below and match each with its opposite meaning. An example has been done for you.

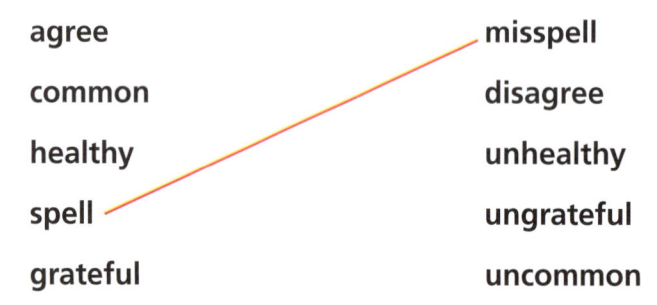

agree	misspell
common	disagree
healthy	unhealthy
spell	ungrateful
grateful	uncommon

2 Write out the words below with prefixes. An example has been done for you.

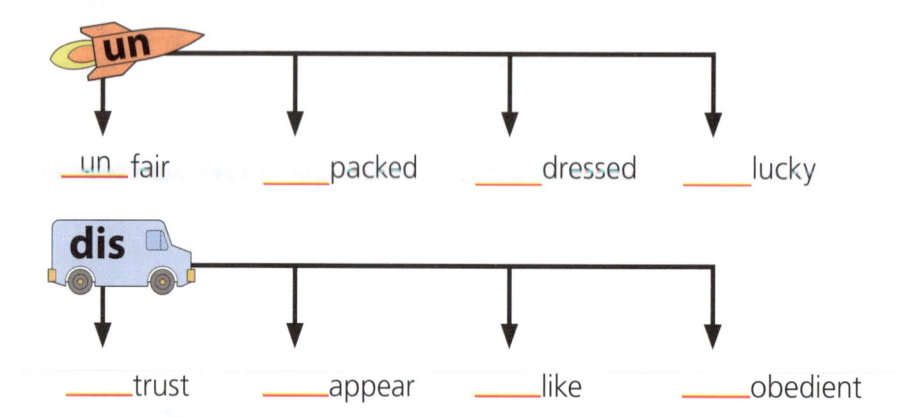

un
- _un_ fair
- ____ packed
- ____ dressed
- ____ lucky

dis
- ____ trust
- ____ appear
- ____ like
- ____ obedient

Test yourself

3 Add **un–**, **dis–** or **mis–** to these words to change their meaning.

a) tidy
b) guide
c) courage
d) appoint
e) true
f) grace
g) behave
h) pleasant
i) obey
j) lead
k) charge
l) common

Challenge yourself

4 Write out the sentences below and add the prefix **un–**, **dis–** or **mis–** to each underlined word to change the meaning of each sentence.

a) I was very lucky.
b) Magicians make rabbits appear.
c) The children were behaving.
d) I trust what you say.
e) I like sprouts.

How did you do?

Progress test 1

Choose the correct spelling of each word.

1. people / peepul
2. becorz / because
3. gud / good
4. Febuary / February
5. bushes / bushs

Write the correct spelling for each word.

6. dishees
7. occured
8. gardning
9. unnpleasant
10. disbehave

Write the correct spelling for each underlined word.

11. Tomorrow, I will <u>beginn</u> my homework project.
12. When I was younger, I <u>preferrd</u> vanilla ice cream.
13. Everyone tried to <u>heid</u> behind the wall.
14. They <u>bilt</u> a den in the garden.
15. Fresh <u>bred</u> is baked daily.

16–20. Read the **passage** below. Find the **five** incorrect spellings and then write down the correct spelling of each word.

> He left his bedroom very unntidy every day. His mother would cleen it and put the toys in their boxs.
>
> She was dissappointed that he could dissobey her.

Score ◯ / 20

16

Progress test 2

Choose the correct spelling of each word.

1. January / Janury
2. mis's / misses
3. foxes / foxs
4. exclamed / exclaimed
5. jumped / jumpt

Write the correct spelling for each word.

6. prefferring
7. unavoydable
8. dissappear
9. untroo
10. missleading

Write the correct spelling for each underlined word.

11. Dad was cross because the children were ungreatful.
12. All of the glas's were filled with lemonade.
13. In a centry, there are one hundred years.
14. Orgust is the eighth month of the year.
15. The choir were singing twogether.

16–20. Read the passage below. Find the **five** incorrect spellings and then write down the correct spelling of each word.

> The hed coach of the teem sat on a stule and read a buk while the players trained in the medow.

Score ◯/20

Plural endings

When a noun ends with **f** or **fe**, you usually change the **f** or **fe** to **v** and add **es** to make it plural.

one loaf   two loa**ves**

When a noun ends with a **vowel + y**, you usually add **s** to make it plural.

one monkey   two monkey**s**

When a noun ends with a **consonant + y**, you change the **y** to **i** and add **es**.

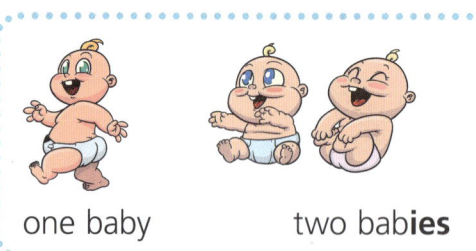

one baby   two bab**ies**

Warm up

1 Write down the plural of these nouns.

key	**lorry**
trolley	**toy**
guy	**berry**
cry	**pulley**

2 Write down the singular of these nouns.

flies	**boys**
copies	**ladies**
days	**bodies**
cherries	**turkeys**

Test yourself

3 Copy and complete the table. An example has been done for you.

singular	plural
leaf	leaves
half	
thief	
shelf	
knife	
	wives
	wolves
	calves
	lives
	elves

Challenge yourself

4 Rewrite these sentences correctly.

Each sentence contains one spelling mistake.

a) All turkies gobble.
b) London and Paris are citys.
c) The baker made lots of loafs.
d) We picked some berrys off the bush.
e) A pack of wolfs lives in the woods.

How did you do?

The suffix –ly

Look what happens when you add **ly** to some adjectives to make them into adverbs:

quick + **ly** = quick**ly**   cold + **ly** = cold**ly**
bad + **ly** = bad**ly**   amazing + **ly** = amazing**ly**

Warm up

1 Add **–ly** to these words. Write the new word.

sudden	**complete**
quiet	**smart**
slow	**mad**
loud	**stupid**
loving	**late**
hopeful	**annoying**

Test yourself

2 Take the suffix off each adverb. Write the adjectives you are left with.

gladly	cheaply
nicely	willingly
proudly	calmly
slowly	quickly
wickedly	sadly
cleverly	smartly
madly	highly

Challenge yourself

3 Copy and complete each sentence by adding the appropriate adverb.

> **Example**
> The bride walked _____ down the aisle. (She was slow.)
> The bride walked <u>slowly</u> down the aisle.

a) Paul ran _____ to school. (He was quick.)

b) _____, the boy peeped around the corner (He was cautious.)

c) _____, the team captain lifted the cup. (It was a proud moment.)

d) Karl had _____ swapped his old car for a newer model. (He was glad.)

e) _____, they helped the coach driver to load the luggage. (They were willing.)

f) He _____ calculated the answer in his head. (He was clever.)

How did you do?

21

Words with ge and dge

Apart from at the beginning of words, as in **j**am or **j**ump, **j** is rarely used to make the **j** sound. When it immediately follows a short vowel sound, it is spelt **dge**. If it follows a long vowel sound, or a consonant, the **j** sound is spelt **ge**.

Examples:

he**dge**   hu**ge**

Warm up

1. Copy and complete these **dge** words.

   he_____   le_____   tru_____   bu_____

2. Copy and complete these **ge** words.

   oran_____   hu_____   a_____   bul_____

3. Identify the **ge** and **dge** words below. Write them out and underline the letters that make the **j** sound.

   garage   gadget   badge   kitchen
   hedgehog   fudge   latch   wage

Answers

Pages 4–5
1. a) sed/said
    b) beecuz/because
    c) peepul/people
    d) wud/would
    e) muther/mother
    f) litul/little
    g) sanwij/sandwich
2. a) boat
    b) purse
    c) moon
    d) mouse
    e) light f) torch g) paint h) bird
3. a) shoes
    b) climb
    c) pretty
    d) kind
    e) hour
    f) floor
    g) laugh

Pages 6–7
1. neat, heap, speak, team, beach
2. read, deaf, sweat, weather, meadow
3. food, stool, hoop, proof, broom
4. good, book, foot, stood, shook
5. a) cube
    b) rode
    c) ripe
    d) code
    e) pipe
    f) hate
    g) fine
    h) shine
6. a) hot = S, day = L
    b) They = L, made = L, den = S
    c) Rain = L, soaking = L
    d) had = S, long = S, flowing = L, cape = L
    e) went = S, run = S, park = L

Pages 8–9
1. modern 2, invade 2, cabin 2, king 1, determine 3, sport 1, together 3, introduce 3, industry 3, seat 1, expensive 3, September 3, travel 2, habit 2, method 2, direct 2, farm 1, bird 1
2. century 3, decade 2, millennium 4, year 1, fortnight 2, eternity 4, forever 3, lifetime 2
3. a) Monday, Tuesday, Thursday, Friday, Sunday, Wednesday
    b) Saturday
4. a) March, May, June
    b) April, July, August
    c) September, October, November, December
    d) January, February
5. Responses will vary but the number of syllables and the spelling must be correct.

Pages 10–11
1. dish/dishes; kiss/kisses; cat/cats; coach/coaches; fox/foxes; song/songs; boss/bosses; tree/trees; six/sixes; catch/catches; bus/buses; miss/misses
2. a) dresses
    b) bushes
    c) horse
    d) benches
    e) carpet
    f) windows
    g) bus
    h) pizza
3. a) splashes
    b) sheep
    c) moons
    d) potatoes
    e) glasses
    f) coaches
    g) sixes
    h) houses

Pages 12–13
1. jump, garden, call, camp
2. preferred, visited, exclaimed, hovered, occurred, begged
3. a) When I was in Year 1, I always preferred to have a hot school dinner.
    b) Two years ago, the same argument always occurred at the bus stop.
    c) The children begged for every penny they raised.
    d) There is a limited range of goods for sale.
    e) The teenagers had trouble admitting they were wrong.
    f) Sunbathing is relaxing, but not if it is too hot.
4. **Sentences must include selected words from below, used in the correct context.**
    a) relaxed, relaxing
    b) gardener, gardening
    c) beginner, beginning
    d) played, player, playing

Pages 14–15
1. agree   disagree
   common   uncommon
   healthy   unhealthy
   spell   misspell
   grateful   ungrateful
2. un- unfair, unpacked, undressed, unlucky
   dis- distrust, disappear, dislike, disobedient
3. a) untidy
    b) misguide
    c) discourage
    d) disappoint
    e) untrue
    f) disgrace
    g) misbehave

1

Answers

    h) unpleasant
    i) disobey
    j) mislead
    k) discharge
    l) uncommon
4. a) unlucky
    b) disappear
    c) misbehaving
    d) distrust/mistrust
    e) dislike

Page 16: Progress Test 1
1. people
2. because
3. good
4. February
5. bushes
6. dishes
7. occurred
8. gardening
9. unpleasant
10. misbehave
11. begin
12. preferred
13. hide
14. built
15. bread
16.–20. **The following five words can be written in any order:**
    untidy, clean, boxes, disappointed, disobey

Page 17: Progress Test 2
1. January
2. misses
3. foxes
4. exclaimed
5. jumped
6. preferring
7. unavoidable
8. disappear
9. untrue
10. misleading
11. ungrateful
12. glasses
13. century
14. August
15. together
16.–20. **The following five words can be written in any order:**
    head, team, book, stool, meadow

Pages 18–19
1. keys, lorries, trolleys, toys, guys, berries, cries, pulleys
2. fly, boy, copy, lady, day, body, cherry, turkey
3. leaf/leaves; half/halves; thief/thieves; shelf/shelves; knife/knives; wife/wives; wolf/wolves; calf/calves; life/lives; elf/elves

4. a) All turkeys gobble.
    b) London and Paris are cities.
    c) The baker made lots of loaves.
    d) We picked some berries off the bush.
    e) A pack of wolves lives in the woods.

Pages 20–21
1. suddenly, completely, quietly, smartly, slowly, madly, loudly, stupidly, lovingly, lately, hopefully, annoyingly
2. glad, cheap, nice, willing, proud, calm, slow, quick, wicked, sad, clever, smart, mad, high
3. a) quickly
    b) Cautiously
    c) Proudly
    d) gladly
    e) Willingly
    f) cleverly

Pages 22–23
1. hedge, ledge, trudge, budge
2. orange, huge, age, bulge
3. gara<u>ge</u>, ga<u>dg</u>et, ba<u>dge</u>, he<u>dge</u>hog, fu<u>dge</u>, wa<u>ge</u> (not kitchen and latch)
4. a) bridge b) dodgem/dodge c) badger d) barge
5. a) sledging
    b) charging
    c) villager
    d) lodger
    e) bulging
    f) oranges
    g) barge
    h) hedgehog
    i) badge

Pages 24–25
1. vague, technique, synagogue, colleague, boutique
2. a) league – a group of teams or organisations competing or working together
    b) antique – something old, from the past
    c) unique – the only one of its kind
3. a) colleague   b) intrigue
    c) technique   d) meringue
    e) fatigue   f) unique
    g) vague   h) antique
4. A complete sentence must be written for each word, with the selected word used in the correct context.
    a) plague or plaque
    b) opaque
    c) epilogue
    d) boutique
    e) mosque
    f) catalogue
    g) cheque
    h) discotheque
    i) dialogue
    j) picturesque

Answers

Pages 26–27
1. vein, weigh, obey, eight, freight, hey, prey, veil, survey, they, sleigh, grey, reign, neighbour, convey, reindeer
2. a) great, prey
   b) veil, face
   c) They, cake
   d) always, obey
   e) Eight, place
   f) say, age
   g) survey, late
   h) neighbour, grey
3. Sentences will vary, but they must contain the stated word with the correct spelling, be correctly punctuated and make sense.

Pages 28–29
1. stir, term, purse, church
2. play, eight, weigh, sail
3. boiled, soil, loyal, enjoy
4. a) their
   b) There
   c) there
   d) their
5. a) too
   b) to
   c) two
   d) too, to
6. a) break
   b) grate
   c) ate
   d) wait
   e) sun

Page 30: Progress Test 3
1. snail
2. unique
3. bridge
4. delay
5. hopefully
6. gently
7. charge
8. copies
9. gadget
10. dodge
11. hear
12. knight
13. There
14. weather
15. hear
16.–20. The following five words can be written in any order:
    neighbour, colleague, suddenly, athletically, guys

Page 31: Progress Test 4
1. badge
2. village
3. league
4. technique
5. intrigue
6. babies
7. basically
8. huge
9. survey
10. quickly
11. weigh
12. antique
13. monkeys
14. eight
15. hedgehog
16.–20. The following five words can be written in any order:
    sadly, ladies, plaque, happily, sleigh

Pages 32–33
1. a) international
   b) autobiography
   c) supermarket
   d) reappear
   e) antiseptic
   f) automatic
   g) unrelated
   h) return
   i) redo
   j) submarine
2. a) superman
   b) reappear
   c) automatic
   d) antidote
   e) intercity
   f) submerge
3. A range of words are possible, many from pages 32–33. Check responses using a dictionary.
4. Prefixes and sentences will vary. Sentences must contain the stated prefix with correct spelling, be correctly punctuated and make sense.

Pages 34–35
1. *k* sound: school, stomach, character, anchor, chemist, ache, chaos, architect; *sh* sound: brochure, chef, machine, moustache, parachute, chauffeur
2. machine, chemist, moustache, brochure, anchor, chalet, chorus, chef
3. a) school
   b) echo
   c) character
   d) chorus
   e) chauffeur
   f) machine
   g) anchor
   h) chef
   i) chemist

3

Answers

Pages 36–37
1. crystal, cymbal, Egypt, hymn, mystery, oxygen, typical
2. a) gym
   b) syrup
   c) symbol
   d) myth
   e) symptom
3. a) mystery
   b) syllable
   c) pyramids, Egyptians
   d) cymbal
   e) oxygen
   f) system
   g) lyrics
4. a) winter
   b) infant
   c) myth
   d) silly
   e) crystal
   f) cylinder
   g) gymnastics
   h) physics
   i) symptom
   j) lyrics
   k) crypt
   l) cygnet
   m) calypso
   n) symphony

Pages 38–39
1. u words: umbrella, butter, fund, supply
   ou words: encourage, cousin, nourish, touch
2. young, supper, trouble, country, thunder
3. **Across:** couple, country, rough
   Down: courage, young
4. Sentences will vary, but they must contain one of the stated words with the correct spelling, be correctly punctuated and make sense.

Pages 40–41
1. accept/except; ball/bawl; not/knot; allowed/aloud; hear/here; plain/plane
2. a) knows
   b) heal
   c) plane
   d) grown
   e) accept
   f) mist
3. Sentences will vary, but they must contain the stated word with the correct spelling, be correctly punctuated and make sense.
4. Sentences will vary, but they must contain one of the stated words with the correct spelling, be correctly punctuated and make sense.

Page 42: Progress Test 5
1. cousin
2. pyramid
3. character
4. submerge
5. antiseptic
6. rough
7. myth
8. brochure
9. country
10. crystal
11. oxygen
12. touch
13. through
14. berry
15. heel
16.–20. The following five words can be written in any order:
    young, break, pieces, not, allowed

Page 43: Progress Test 6
1. mystery
2. reappear
3. gymnastics
4. machine
5. enough
6. chemist
7. school
8. trouble
9. automatic
10. parachute
11. international
12. plain
13. accept
14. courage
15. mist
16.–20. The following five words can be written in any order:
    heard, stomach, groan, chef, double

4

Test yourself

4 Look at each picture and write out the **dge** or **ge** word.

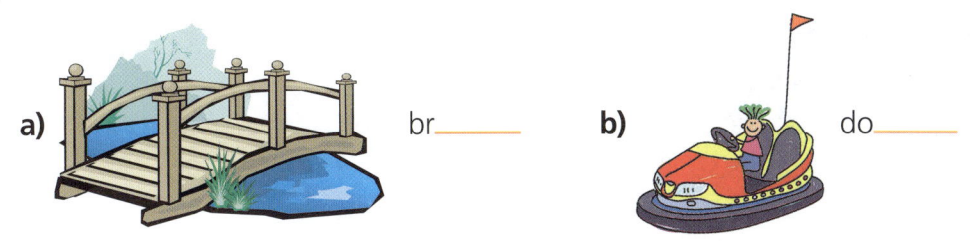

a) br_____

b) do_____

c) ba_____

d) ba_____

Challenge yourself

5 Copy and complete each sentence below with a **ge** or **dge** word.

Be careful – the ending of the word may need to be changed (see pages 12 and 13).

a) When it snows, find a hill and go sl_____.

b) We tried to cross the field but the bull kept ch_____ us.

c) Someone who lives in a very small town is known as a vi_____.

d) A lo_____ is someone who pays to live in another person's house.

e) The bag was so full it was bu_____.

f) Or_____ are fruit full of vitamin C.

g) The ba_____ transported the goods along the river.

h) The he_____ has lots of prickles to defend itself.

i) The school council members all wore a special ba_____.

How did you do?

-gue and -que from French

Many English words and spellings originate from France.

Words ending with a **g** sound (as in **g**ap) are sometimes spelt with a **–gue** ending.

fati**gue**

Words ending with a **k** sound (as in **k**id) are sometimes spelt with a **–que** ending.

mos**que**

Warm up

1 Using the sounds described above, write out the words that might have a French origin.

ring   **vague**   **technique**   **synagogue**

kick   **colleague**   **log**   **boutique**

2 Write a definition for each of the words below.

Use a dictionary to help you.

a) league

b) antique

c) unique

Test yourself

3 Choose **–gue** or **–que** to copy and complete each word.

Say the word aloud to help you listen for the 'g' and 'k' sounds at the end of each word.

a) collea_____   b) intri_____
c) techni_____   d) merin_____
e) fati_____   f) uni_____
g) va_____   h) anti_____

Challenge yourself

4 Copy and complete the words below with **–gue** or **–que**.

Write a sentence for each word.

Use a dictionary to check the meaning.

(**pla–** can have either **–gue** or **–que** added.)

a) pla_____
b) opa_____
c) epilo_____
d) bouti_____
e) mos_____
f) catalo_____
g) che_____
h) discothe_____
i) dialo_____
j) pictures_____

How did you do?

Words with ei, eigh and ey

The letter patterns **ei**, **eigh** and **ey** often make the long **a** sound, as in g**a**me.

Examples:

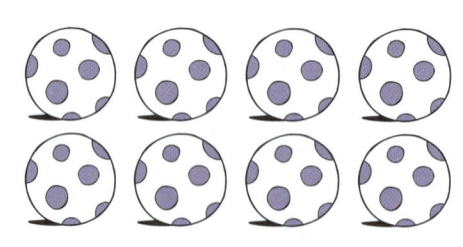

How much do I w**eigh**?   **Eigh**t balls   Gr**ey**hound

There is no rule for these spelling patterns. They just have to be learned.

Warm up

1 Write down the words in which **ei**, **eigh** or **ey** make the long **a** sound.

Be careful – some words are included to trick you!

vein	play	state	weigh
day	obey	eight	height
foray	freight	hey	prey
clay	delay	veil	snail
survey	their	rate	they
sleigh	grey	rain	reign
neighbour	convey	reindeer	holiday

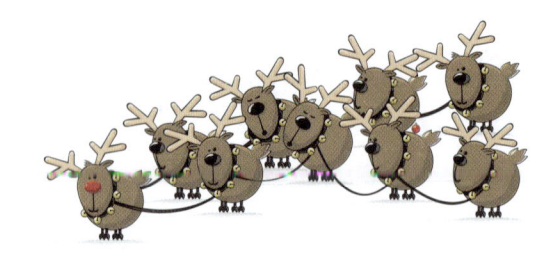

Test yourself

2 Identify and write down two words containing the long **a** sound in each of these sentences.

   a) The great beast stalked his prey.
   b) The veil covered the bride's face.
   c) They eat their cake at lunchtime.
   d) You must always obey the rules.
   e) Eight girls liked the place.
   f) Some say 'age before beauty'.
   g) The survey was finished late.
   h) The neighbour had grey hair.

Challenge yourself

3 Write sentences containing each of these words.

   a) weigh
   b) vein
   c) they
   d) neighbour
   e) reindeer
   f) freight
   g) sleigh
   h) obey

How did you do?

Different spelling, same sound

Take care! Many words contain the same or similar sounds, but have different spelling patterns.

Example:

a n**ur**se in a sk**ir**t with a lant**er**n

In this example, the **ur**, **ir** and **er** spellings can easily be confused.

Warm up

1 Identify the **er**, **ir** or **ur** sound in each of the words below. An example has been done for you.

stir ⟶ st<u>ir</u>

term

purse

church

2 Identify the **ai**, **eigh** or **ay** sound in each of the words below.

play

eight

weigh

sail

3 Identify the **oi** or **oy** sound in each of the words below.

boiled

soil

loyal

enjoy

Test yourself

4 Decide whether to use **there** or **their** in each sentence.

a) It was _____ house.

b) _____ is always sunshine on holiday.

c) She was always _____ waiting for him.

d) They could not believe _____ luck.

5 Decide whether to use **to**, **too** or **two** to complete each sentence.

a) We would like to come _____.

b) I am going _____ the park.

c) There are only _____ minutes until playtime.

d) Is it _____ late _____ buy a ticket?

Challenge yourself

6 Choose the correct word in bold to complete each sentence.

a) The glass will **brake / break** if dropped.

b) The log was burning in the fire **grate / great**.

c) It was very late when they **ate / eight**.

d) After a long **wait / weight** they finally saw the Queen.

e) It was incredibly hot in the **son / sun**.

How did you do?

Progress test 3

Choose the correct spelling of each word below.

1. snail / snale
2. uneeq / unique
3. brigde / bridge
4. deley / delay
5. hopefully / hopefulley

Write the correct spelling for each word.

6. gentally
7. chardge
8. copys
9. gajet
10. dodgje

Write the correct spelling for each underlined word.

11. The <u>bare</u> was attracted to the honey in the nest.
12. Gawain was a brave <u>night</u> of the Round Table.
13. <u>Their</u> were six of them on the bouncy castle.
14. Outside, the <u>whether</u> was awful.
15. She could hardly <u>here</u> a sound from the classroom.

16–20. Read the passage below. Find the **five** incorrect spellings and then write the correct spelling of each word.

> **To my neybour's surprise, my colleeg suddenely jumped athleticlly and grabbed the bad guies.**

Score ◯/20

Progress test 4

Choose the correct spelling of each word below.

1. badge / badj
2. villige / village
3. leeg / league
4. teckneek / technique
5. intrigue / intrig

Write the correct spelling for each word.

6. babys
7. basicly
8. huje
9. survay
10. quikerly

Write the correct spelling for each underlined word.

11. They found the scales to way the fish.
12. In the attic, was a rare anteeqe.
13. The monkys were swinging in the trees.
14. Only ate cakes were eaten at the party.
15. To protect itself, the hedjhog rolled into a ball.

16 – 20. Read the passage below. Find the **five** incorrect spellings and then write the correct spelling of each word.

> **Sadley, the dentist told the four ladys they all had lots of plack on their teeth. Happerly, they were able to get a free ride home on a super, horse-drawn slay which made them feel happier.**

Score ◯/20

Prefixes 2: A variety of meanings

Prefixes can have many different meanings. Some, such as **un–** and **dis–**, change the word to its opposite meaning. Here are the meanings of some other prefixes:

> **re–** means 'again' or 'back', e.g. **re**turn.
> **sub–** means 'under', e.g. **sub**side.
> **inter–** means 'between' or 'among', e.g. **inter**lock.
> **super–** means 'above', e.g. **super**sonic.
> **anti–** means 'against', e.g. **anti**bacterial.
> **auto–** means 'self' or 'own', e.g. **auto**pilot.

Warm up

1 Use the correct prefix to make these words match the definitions. Write out the new words.

a) Between nations　　　　　　　　　　_____national

b) My own biography　　　　　　　　　_____biography

c) Bigger than a small market or shop　_____market

d) Appear again　　　　　　　　　　　 _____appear

e) Preventing becoming septic　　　　 _____septic

f) Happens by itself　　　　　　　　　 _____matic

g) Not related to each other　　　　　 _____related

h) Come back　　　　　　　　　　　　_____turn

i) Do something again　　　　　　　　_____do

j) An underwater vessel　　　　　　　 _____marine

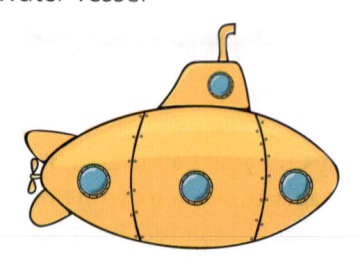

32

Test yourself

2 Match the prefix to the root word and write down the new words. An example has been done for you.

- **a)** super — dote
- **b)** re — city
- **c)** auto — appear
- **d)** anti — man
- **e)** inter — merge
- **f)** sub — matic

Challenge yourself

3 Write as many words as you can find for each prefix.

Use a dictionary to help you.

- **a)** re–
- **b)** sub–
- **c)** inter–
- **d)** super–
- **e)** anti–
- **f)** auto–

4 Think of the prefix to add to each of the words below, then write a sentence containing each word.

- **a)** sonic
- **b)** bacterial
- **c)** pilot
- **d)** national
- **e)** way
- **f)** market
- **g)** matic
- **h)** septic

How did you do?

33

ch from different languages

English uses lots of spellings from different languages.

Examples:

Sometimes the **k** sound (as in **k**it) is spelt **ch**.

s**ch**ool

This spelling originates from Greek.

Sometimes the **sh** sound (as in **sh**op) is spelt **ch**.

chef

This spelling often has French origins.

Warm up

1 Copy out this table and rewrite the **ch** words under the correct headings.

brochure   school   stomach   character   chef
anchor   machine   chemist   ache   chaos
moustache   parachute   chauffeur   architect

ch making a *k* sound	ch making a *sh* sound

Test yourself

2 Rewrite each word with the correct spelling.

mashine

kemist

moustashe

broshure

ankor

shalet

korus

shef

Challenge yourself

3 Write the correct **ch** word for each definition.
Check your answers using a dictionary.

a) Where children are educated.

b) A sound reflected from a surface.

c) A person in a book or a film.

d) Part of a song.

e) Somebody who drives people around.

f) A mechanical tool for making things.

g) A heavy object to stop a ship floating away.

h) Sometimes referred to as a cook.

i) A person who experiments with chemicals.

How did you do?

Using y to spell the short *i* sound

Sometimes the short *i* sound (as in b**i**g) is spelt using a **y**.

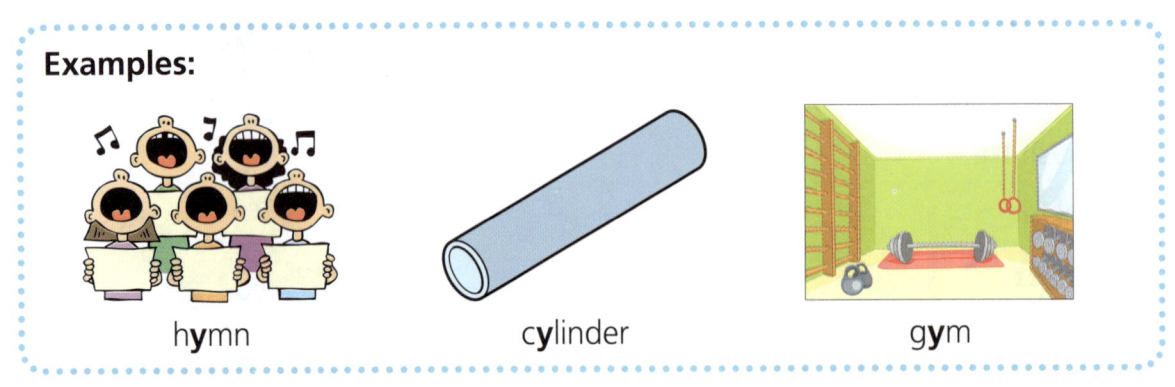

Examples:

h**y**mn   c**y**linder   g**y**m

These do not follow a rule. You just have to become familiar with words containing this spelling.

Warm up

1) Rewrite the list of words in alphabetical order.

mystery
typical
crystal
hymn
Egypt
oxygen
cymbal

2) Correct the following words by rewriting them using a **y** for the short *i* sound.

a) gim

b) sirup

c) simbol

d) mith

e) simptom

Test yourself

3 Identify the correct word from the list below to complete each sentence.

Use a dictionary if you are unsure of the meaning of any of the words.

mystery	lyrics	cymbal	system
oxygen	pyramids	syllable	Egyptians

a) Nobody knew how to solve the _____ of the missing diamond.

b) Each beat in a spoken word is called a _____.

c) The _____ were built by the ancient _____.

d) The drumstick broke when the drummer struck the _____.

e) _____ is an essential gas which animals need to breathe.

f) The Sun is at the centre of the solar _____.

g) She could not get the song _____ out of her head.

Challenge yourself

4 Decide whether a **y** or **i** should be inserted into each space to make the short *i* sound. Write out each word with the correct spelling.

Use a dictionary to check whether you have chosen correctly.

a) w__nter
b) __nfant
c) s__lly
d) cr__stal
e) g__mnast__cs
f) ph__s__cs
g) l__r__c
h) cr__pt
i) cal__pso
j) s__mphony
k) m__th
l) s__mptom
m) c__l__nder
n) c__gnet

How did you do?

When ou spells the u sound

Some words in which you hear the short **u** sound (as in m**u**g) use the spelling **ou**.

Examples:

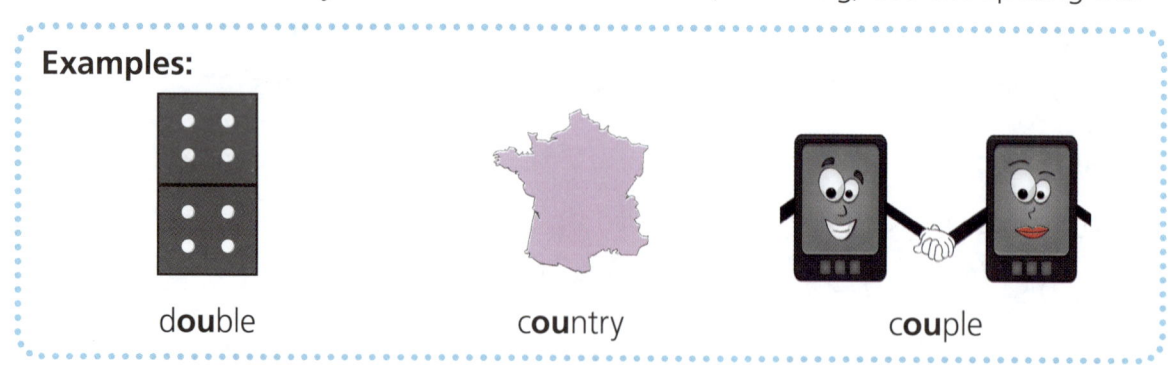

d**ou**ble   c**ou**ntry   c**ou**ple

This is another spelling which just has to be learned. There is no rule, so you have to remember words which are spelt in this way.

Warm up

1 Copy and complete the table by writing words from the list into the correct column.

| umbrella | encourage | cousin | butter |
| fund | nourish | supply | touch |

u words	ou words

2 Copy and complete the following words with either **ou** or **u**.

Check using a dictionary.

y____ng   s____pper   tr____ble   c____ntry   th____nder

Test yourself

3 What are the missing words? Write them out in full.

			c			p	l	e
	c			n	t	r	y	
			r					
			a					
r			g	h			n	
			e				g	

Challenge yourself

4 Write sentences containing at least one word from each pair of words.

a) cousin, young

b) trouble, rough

c) courage, touch

d) couple, country

e) encourage, enough

f) flourish, nourishment

How did you do?

39

Homophones

Homophones are words that sound the same, but have different meanings.

Examples:

I **heard** a noise

a **herd** of cattle

Near-homophones are words that sound similar and are often confused when spelt, e.g. **advise** and **advice**.

Warm up

1. Copy these words and match up the pairs of homophones and near-homophones. An example has been done for you.

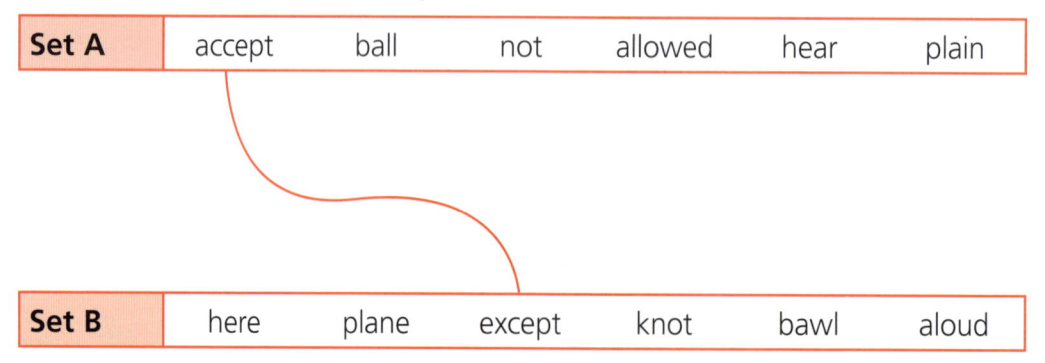

| Set A | accept | ball | not | allowed | hear | plain |

| Set B | here | plane | except | knot | bawl | aloud |

2. Choose the correct word to complete each sentence. An example has been done for you.

   a) The pirate **nose / knows** where the treasure is.

   b) The cut in her leg was starting to **heel / heal / he'll**.

   c) The **plain / plane** made quite a noise on take-off.

   d) After a few days the beans had **groan / grown**.

   e) He would not **accept / except** that the game was lost.

   f) We saw the top of the castle above the **missed / mist**.

Test yourself

3 Write sentences using the given homophones.

Use a dictionary to help you to understand the meaning of each word.

a) groan

b) grown

c) knot

d) not

e) aloud

f) allowed

Challenge yourself

4 Write a sentence for each of these homophones.

a) berry

b) bury

c) rain

d) reign

e) threw

f) through

g) there

h) their

i) they're

How did you do?

Progress test 5

Choose the correct spelling of each word below.

1. cousin / cusern
2. piramid / pyramid
3. character / caracter
4. supmerge / submerge
5. antyseptic / antiseptic

Write the correct spelling for each word.

6. ruff
7. mith
8. broasher
9. cunchry
10. cristal

Write the correct spelling for each underlined word.

11. The dive was cut short because they were low on <u>oxigen</u>.
12. Nobody was allowed to <u>tuch</u> the famous statue.
13. Rain was falling <u>threw</u> the hole in the roof.
14. Every <u>bury</u> was eaten by the hungry birds.
15. She fell when the <u>he'll</u> of her shoe snapped.

16 – 20. Read the passage below. Find the **five** incorrect spellings and then write the correct spelling of each word.

> **The yung boy was told that he couldn't brake the jigsaw into peaces. His sister had done it and he was knot aloud to play with her toys.**

Score /20

Progress test 6

Choose the correct spelling of each word below.

1. mistery / mystery
2. reeappear / reappear
3. gimnastics / gymnastics
4. machine / mashine
5. enough / enuff

Write the correct spelling for each word.

6. cemist
7. scool
8. trubble
9. ortomatic
10. parashoot

Write the correct spelling for each underlined word.

11. They were on the next <u>internashnul</u> flight.
12. Her dress was very <u>plane</u>.
13. She could not <u>except</u> that it was a goal.
14. The zookeeper had great <u>curryage</u> to go into the lion enclosure.
15. A beautiful layer of <u>missed</u> lay over the lake.

16–20. Read the passage below. Find the **five** incorrect spellings and then write the correct spelling of each word.

> I herd my stumack grown. The shef had made a rich dessert and I'd managed dubble helpings.

Score ◯/20

Published by Keen Kite Books
An imprint of HarperCollins*Publishers* Ltd
The News Building, 1 London Bridge Street,
London, SE1 9GF

ISBN 9780008161545

Text and design © 2015 Keen Kite Books, an imprint of HarperCollins*Publishers* Ltd

Author © 2015 Jon Goulding

The author asserts his moral right to be identified as the author of this work.

All rights reserved. No part of this publication may be reproduced, stored in a retrieval system, or transmitted, in any form or by any means, electronic, mechanical, photocopying, recording or otherwise, without the prior permission of HarperCollins*Publishers* Ltd.